# SINCE

# O

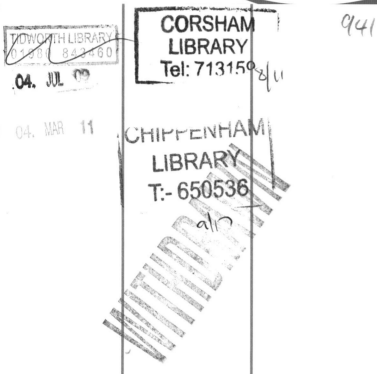

## JANE SHUTER

**Heinemann**

**www.heinemann.co.uk/library**
Visit our website to find out more information about **Heinemann Library** books.

To order:
☎ Phone 44 (0) 1865 888066
 Send a fax to 44 (0) 1865 314091
 Visit the Heinemann Bookshop at www.heinemann.co.uk/library to browse our catalogue and order online.

First published in Great Britain by Heinemann Library, Halley Court, Jordan Hill, Oxford OX2 8EJ, part of Pearson Education.
Heinemann is a registered trademark of Pearson Education Ltd.

Editorial: Jilly Attwood, Kathy Peltan and Vicki Yates
Design: David Poole and Tokay Interactive Ltd
Picture Research: Hannah Taylor
Production: Camilla Smith

Originated by Chroma Graphics (Overseas) Pte. Ltd
Printed and bound in China by
LEO Paper Group

**British Library Cataloguing in Publication Data**
Shuter, Jane
Britain Since 1930
941'.084
A full catalogue record for this book is available from the British Library.

**Acknowledgements**
The publishers would like to thank the following for permission to reproduce photographs:
Alamy Images pp. **26** (Janine Wiedel Photolibrary), **28t** (Tony Hunter); Corbis pp. **21b** (Conde Nast Archive), **27** (Don Mason); Getty Images pp. **5**, **6**, **7**, **8**, **9**, **10**, **13t**, **14**, **16**, **17t** (Hulton Archive), **18** (AFP), **19** (AFP/Gerard Cerles); Harcourt Education Ltd pp. **17b** (Chris Honeywell), **23b**, **23t**, **28b** (Phil Bratt); Imperial War Museum pp. **15t**, **15b**; John Frost Newspapers p. **20**; Rex Features pp. **24**, **25**; The Art Archive p. **12** (Eileen Tweedy); The Robert Opie Collection p. **13b**; V & A Images pp. **21t**, **22**.

Cover photograph of 30 St Mary Axe, reproduced with permission of Alamy Images/Dominic Burke.

The publishers would like to thank Robyn Hardyman, Bob Rees and Caroline Landon for their assistance in the preparation of this book.

Every effort has been made to contact copyright holders of any material reproduced in this book. Any omissions will be rectified in subsequent printings if notice is given to the publishers.

Any words appearing in the text in bold, **like this**, are explained in the glossary.

# Contents

## What was it like for children in the Second World War?

## How has life in Britain changed since 1948?

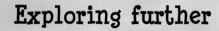

## Exploring further

Throughout the book you will find links to the Heinemann Explore CD-ROM and website

Follow the links to discover more about a topic.

## What do the symbols mean?

The following symbols are used throughout the book:

 Source         See for yourself

 Biography

## What was the Second World War?

The Second World War lasted from 1939 to 1945. It is called a world war because countries from all over the world took part in it. The Second World War took place in many parts of the world, but most of the fighting was in Europe, North Africa, and Asia.

### Europe and North Africa

Germany had lost the First World War (1914–1918). After the war, a lot of land was taken away from Germany. In 1933, the **Nazi Party** came to power in Germany. Its leader was Adolf Hitler. Hitler wanted to get back the land that had been taken away. In 1938, he sent his large army to take it back. Soon, Hitler wanted to take over even more land. Other countries either had to fight on his side, or be ready to fight against him.

Britain and France went to war with Germany in September 1939. This part of the war was mainly fought in Europe and North Africa, on land, at sea, and in the air.

This map shows how much land the Nazis had taken by 1942. This was the largest Germany ever got.

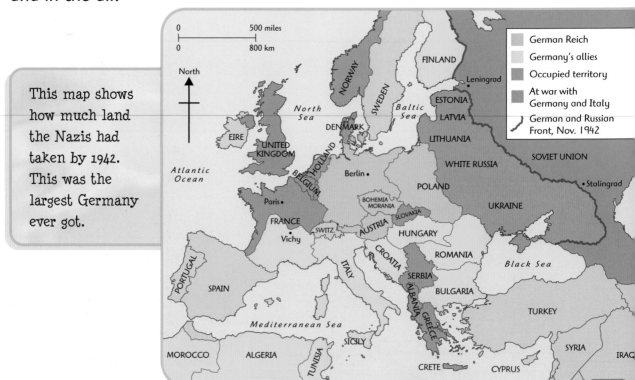

4

## Asia

In Asia, Japan had been trying to take over land in China since 1937. When China's **allies** went to war in Europe, Japan decided to invade China. Then, on 7 December 1941, Japan bombed US ships in Pearl Harbor. The next day, Britain and the USA went to war with Japan. Hitler said that Japan was Germany's ally and the USA was now an enemy.

## The end of the war

The war in Europe ended on 8 May 1945, when Germany **surrendered** to the **Allies**. The war in Asia did not stop until 14 August 1945. It only stopped after two **atomic bombs** had been dropped on Japanese cities – one on Hiroshima and one on Nagasaki.

Adolf Hitler was leader of the German Nazi Party.

## Exploring further

The Heinemann Explore website and CD-ROM include text on all the key topics about Britain since 1930. You will also find pictures, biographies, written sources, and lots of activities to explore. Go to the contents screen. Click on the blue words in the list and off you go!

## Adolf Hitler

Adolf Hitler (1889–1945) was born in Austria. He joined the German Workers' Party in 1919. By 1921, he was in charge. He renamed it the National Socialist German Workers' Party (the Nazi Party for short). By 1932, the Nazi Party was the biggest party in the German **parliament**. Hitler became **Chancellor** in 1933 and quickly passed laws that meant the Nazis were the only party in Germany, and that only he could be its leader. The Nazis spread quickly across Europe. However, in 1944, the Allies began to push the German army back. Hitler was in Berlin. On 29 April 1945, the Russians captured Berlin. Hitler killed himself the next day.

# What was the Blitz?

The **Blitz** is the name given to the heavy bombing of Britain by the German **Luftwaffe** from September 1940 to May 1941. It is a shortened version of the German word 'blitzkrieg' which means 'lightning war'. It was used to describe sudden, heavy attacks. In Britain over 80,000 people were killed in the Blitz.

## Why bomb the cities?

Britain and Germany both bombed each other's cities during the war. They did this to show how powerful they were, to disrupt **communications** and attack industry. They also wanted to scare the people living in the cities and make them want to give up. This did not work. The bombing made most people want to win the war even more.

## Areas that were bombed

Some places were bombed more than others. Towns and cities with ports were badly bombed. This stopped the ships from bringing in and taking out food and weapons. **Factories** were also bombed, so they could not make things for the war.

The **government** thought the Germans would attack with bombs and poison gas. Everyone had to carry a **gas mask** at all times, in case they did.

## What could be done to stop the bombers?

In Britain, people tried to stop the bombers. Guns were set up in cities to shoot down enemy planes. People had to blackout their windows so no lights could be seen outside. Streetlights were turned off. This made it hard for bombers to see where the towns and houses were below them.

One of the most destructive bombing raids was on the city of Coventry, on the night of 14 November 1940. Over 60,000 of the city's 75,000 buildings were destroyed or badly damaged. This picture shows Coventry cathedral which was destroyed. At least 520 people were killed in Coventry that night.

## Winston Churchill

Winston Churchill (1874–1965) became Prime Minister in 1940. Before this he was a Conservative **MP**. He had also fought in the First World War (1914–1918). Before the war, Churchill had warned that the rise of **dictators**, such as Hitler, would lead to another war. During the war, Churchill was a powerful leader. He became famous for the speeches he made to keep people going. After the war ended, Churchill and his government were voted out of power in an election, and the Labour Party took over. The Labour Party made many changes. However, Churchill and the Conservatives were re-elected in 1951. In 1955, Churchill resigned as Prime Minister, but he remained an MP until 1964.

## Exploring further

Use Heinemann Explore CD-ROM, or visit the website to see:

- a video of people clearing debris after the Blitz. Look in 'Media Bank'.

- a personal account of an **air raid** in London. Look in 'Written Sources'.

- statistics of the worst-hit British cities in the Blitz. Look in 'Written Sources'.

# Why were children evacuated?

In 1939 and 1940, the government decided to send children away from cities to keep them safe from the bombing. This would also free their mothers to go out and do war work. Women were needed to take over the jobs of men who were away fighting.

## Where did they go?

Some children went to stay with relatives or friends in the country. Many others were sent to live with strangers, who had volunteered to look after them.

Children who were being evacuated went to school with one case and a packed lunch. They were given a tag with their name on it and put on a train. Many children did not know where they were going to stay.

## Evacuations by sea

Canada and the USA said they would take some **evacuees**. They were safe places to live, but the sea trips were dangerous. The Germans wanted to bomb people to make Britain give up the war. In September 1940, the Germans bombed two sea **evacuation** ships. The children on the first ship were all saved, but only seven evacuees from the second ship survived. There were no more sea evacuations after this.

## How did people in cities try to keep safe?

People with gardens were given a steel **Anderson shelter** to hide in during **air raids**. People without gardens were given a Morrison Shelter. This was used indoors and looked like a table. People taped up their windows to prevent glass flying around. They also put sandbags next to doors and windows to protect them. By May 1941, over 1.4 million people had lost their homes.

During bombing raids many people in London sheltered in underground stations.

## Clearing up

The air raids were mostly at night. During the day, people worked hard repairing the damage. Engineers tried to mend shattered water pipes and electricity cables. The Heavy Rescue Squad worked to clear blocked streets of rubble and overturned vehicles. The most dangerous job of all belonged to the Bomb Disposal Squad. They had to deal with the many bombs and **mines** that hadn't exploded.

## Exploring further

Use the Heinemann Explore CD-ROM, or go to the website to see:

- a video of people sheltering in an underground station during an air raid. Look in 'Media Bank'.

- a video of people living in their Anderson shelter. Look in 'Media Bank'.

- a poster issued by the government to encourage parents not to bring their children back into the cities. Look in 'Pictures, Everyday Life'.

# What was it like to be an evacuee?

Different children had different experiences of life as an **evacuee**. Some children found it hard to be away from their families. Others had a great time. It may have been the first time they had been to the countryside, and they felt safe from the bombs. Many evacuees wrote down or told of their experiences, either at the time or when they were grown up.

## Settling in

Being **evacuated** was a frightening experience for young children. Sometimes brothers and sisters were split up and put in different homes. Sometimes the host families were shocked by the fact that the city children were dirty and had lice or fleas. Sometimes middle-class children found themselves in poor homes, where they had to work hard and sleep on the floor.

The lady in this picture is 'Grannie' Norris. She lived in Kent and took in lots of evacuees. In 1943 she was given a medal for her good work.

L. A. M. Brech, a teacher, remembers being evacuated with her schoolchildren just before war broke out.

*All you could hear was the feet of the children and a kind of murmur because the children were too afraid to talk. Mothers couldn't come with us, but they came along behind. When we got to the station we knew which platform to go to, the train was ready, but we had no idea where we were going. We put the children on the train and the gates closed behind us. The mothers pressed against the iron gates calling 'Goodbye, darling'. I never see those gates at Waterloo without a lump coming to my throat.*

These are parts of two letters, one from Alan Skilton, an evacuee, and one from the mother in his host family. Alan was evacuated to Oldham, in Lancashire, in 1944. He remembers being one of the last children to be chosen. He found it hard to settle down.

*Dear Mum and Dad*
*I like the place and the people, but I would like to come home. I went to the school yesterday but I did not like it as much as our school. Was it hot there yesterday, because it was here. We have no garden to play in. There is a girl living here. I wish I could come home.*

*Dear Mrs Skilton*
*I am sorry Alan is not settling down. He cries rather a lot. I have done everything possible to make them happy, but of course they miss their garden and families.*

Adrian Walker remembers the effect of the evacuees on his village school.

*There was a terrible shortage of space. A lot of evacuee kids had swollen the numbers. They were called 'vacs' or 'vakkies'. We were taught in the church hall across the road as well as at the school. There were two classes in the hall at the same time, with just screens between. They'd be doing singing lessons on one side and trying to teach history on the other.*

Sheila Price was evacuated from London when she was twelve.

*There was an orchard with fruit. We had a car to take us to school, a piano, a beautiful home, servants, typing lessons, mini-golf, and a fine lawn. Most of all, the family was warm and understanding. I became a snob. Each weekend I went home on the bus. Our street looked dingy and poor. I hated it. Eventually, mother said I was to come home and look after the others. My lovely world crumbled.*

# What did people eat during the war?

Before the war, a lot of Britain's food came by ship from other countries. Meat came from Australia, for example, and fruit from the West Indies. During the war, many of the ships were sunk by the Germans so people couldn't get food from other countries. Instead people had to eat food that was only made or grown in Britain. There was often not as much of it as people would have liked.

**POTATOES**
feed without fattening and give you *ENERGY*

## A war meal

During the war, a meal might be a vegetable pie topped with pastry, and a pudding made from rice and dried fruit. People also tried to eat unusual things that grew wild, such as nettles, dandelion and dock leaves. A typical meal during war time was very different to a typical meal before the war.

Posters like this one were produced by the Ministry of Food, to encourage people to eat healthily.

## Rationing and hunger

Most European countries during the war had to have some sort of **rationing**. This limited the amount of certain types of food that people could buy each week. Rationed foods included sugar, butter, cheese, bacon, sweets, and tea. Most people ate less, but the food they did eat was better for them. They ate more vegetables and less fat.

People in Britain always had enough food to keep them going. Some grew their own vegetables. Others kept their own chickens (for eggs), pigs (for meat), or goats (for milk). Some families shared looking after a pig. They all had a share of the meat when it was big enough to eat.

Food was grown wherever possible. Gardens, parks and school playgrounds were useful sites for growing food. Even the moat of the Tower of London was dug over to grow vegetables.

## Exploring further

Use the Heinemann Explore CD-ROM, or visit the website to find out more about:

- how people even grew food in their window boxes. Find a video showing this in 'Media Bank'.

- how people kept animals for meat, milk, and eggs. Look in 'Exploring, Everyday Life.'

- how farmers changed their crops, so as to grow the most useful foods. Look in 'Digging Deeper, The home front'.

This is an average week's ration for one adult during most of the war.

# In what other ways might the war have affected people?

The war changed the lives of people in all sorts of ways. Many men went to fight. Women had to do the work the men would normally do. Some children had to look after themselves, or became **evacuees**. A lot of people had family or friends who were killed in the war, and many lost their homes in the bombings.

## Women and children

Some women took over everyday jobs, such as driving, working on the buses, and delivering milk. Others joined the **Land Army**. This was set up to train women to work on farms. Women also worked in **factories** that made things for the war. Many women also worked in the army, navy, and air force. They could not fight, but they could do other things to help, such as driving ambulances and operating radios.

Many children also joined in with war work. They collected rubbish that could be used again, such as old metal for making airplanes.

Land Girls worked long hours on farms, but were not paid very much.

## Travel

People could not travel much during the war. There were few cars or buses because of petrol **rationing**. Also, many roads and railway lines were bombed. People could not go on holiday, so the **government** encouraged entertainment in towns and workplaces. Music bands played in parks and factories. People also liked to go to the cinema and theatre, and to dances. It helped them to try to forget about the war.

## See for yourself

### Imperial War Museum, London — The Children's War Exhibition

The museum has a major new exhibition that looks at the home front in Britain through the eyes of children. Original letters, diaries, drawings, and photographs, film and spoken recordings tell the story of children's experiences of evacuation, **air raids**, rationing, and the blackout. The 1940s house recreates a typical wartime home, and forms the centrepiece of a hands-on gallery, where visitors can learn about everyday life on the home front.

# What were children's experiences of the war?

Children in different countries had different experiences of the war. This depended on where they lived. In areas taken over by the Germans, it also depended on their religion.

## British children

Growing up in Britain during the war was often hard. **Evacuated** children were separated from their mothers. Many children's fathers were away fighting. Many children were killed or hurt during the bombing raids.

While their parents were working, many children played on bomb sites, even though they were told not to. Some bombs were painted bright colours to make children want to pick them up.

## Jewish children

In countries that the Germans controlled Jewish people had a very bad time during the war. The Germans put them, and other people who they thought were 'inferior', such as gypsies, in camps. There they had to work very hard, and were given very little food. Many were killed in **death camps** set up in Poland.

Some Jewish people fled to other countries to get away from the Germans. Some came to Britain, where they were safe. Those who went to Holland or France were not safe, as the Germans soon took over there.

Hundreds of thousands of Jewish children died in the war, many in the camps. Those who survived lost many members of their family.

## Anne Frank

Anne Frank (1929–1945) was born in Germany. Anne and her parents (Otto and Edith) and her sister Margot moved to Amsterdam, Holland when the Nazis came to power. In 1940 the Nazis took over Holland as well. Otto Frank made a secret hiding place, called the Annexe, in the offices over his warehouse. The Franks moved into the Annexe in July 1942, and lived there for two years. Anne kept a diary of the experience, which we can read today. On 4 July 1944, the Nazis discovered the Annexe. They put the Franks and their friends in a Dutch prison camp. Then they were moved to Auschwitz camp in German-occupied Poland. Anne's mother died in Auschwitz. Anne and Margot were moved to Belsen camp in Germany, where they both died, just before the **Allies** freed the camp. Otto was the only survivor from the Annexe.

## What was life like during the Second World War in your area?

You can find information about the war in your area at local museums, County Record Offices, and at public libraries. They should have photos, maps, and written records. You might also ask older people who remember the war to tell you about their experiences.

# What has been done since to prevent another world war?

The Second World War ended in 1945. Millions of people had been killed, and many areas were devastated. With the invention of the powerful **atomic bomb**, people knew that a future war would be even more destructive. It must not be allowed to happen.

## The United Nations

After the war, Germany and other countries joined an organization called the **United Nations** (UN). It was set up to stop war between countries. It wanted countries to try to talk things through instead of fighting with each other. The first job the UN had to do was try and get Europe back to normal life. Many **refugees** needed help to find their homes and families.

Soldiers of the UN form a 'peacekeeping' force in areas where there has been fighting. These soldiers are in the Democratic Republic of Congo.

## The UN today

After the war, the UN had 50 member countries; today it has over 100. The UN works to try to stop countries from fighting, and to help poorer countries in need. It helps them by sending medical help, giving them clean water, and showing people the best way to farm land or dig wells for clean water.

This is from the United Nations' Charter.

*We, the peoples of the United Nations, are determined to save future generations from war and to reaffirm our faith in human rights.*

## The European Union

To prevent another war happening in Europe, many countries have joined together to form the European Union (EU). Countries in the EU agree to work together on matters such as trade and making laws that will apply to all the members.

Countries in Europe now work together. Here the European Parliament is meeting to discuss important matters.

## Exploring further

Use the Heinemann Explore CD-ROM, or go to the website to find out more about:

- the role of the UN in world crises since 1945. Look in 'Written Sources'.

- an example of the work of the World Health Organization. Look in 'Written Sources'.

## A peaceful world?

There has been no world war since 1945, but that does not mean there is no more war. There is always a war going on somewhere in the world. A lot more work still needs to be done to stop wars from happening.

# How can we begin to find out about change since the Second World War?

It is now over 60 years since the end of the Second World War, and Britain today is a very different place. The buildings and countryside look different. People have changed too. There are now many more people from different races, and we wear very different clothes from the 1940s. Our jobs, schools and family life would all surprise a person living in the 1940s.

## The speed of change

Some of the changes have been slow, others have been fast. Changes in technology have been fastest since the 1960s. A person living in the 1940s would find it difficult to work many of the things we have in our homes today, such as computers, televisions, even irons!

## So much change

When looking at changes since 1945, there are many areas and several time periods to consider. This can be confusing. It is easiest to choose just one **decade**, such as the 1950s or the 1970s. Then pick one area of change at a time, such as technology, work, homes, or the population. Ask yourself questions such as: 'What has changed? What has stayed the same? Why have so many changes occurred?'

Newspapers tell us about important events in the past. They also show what was important to people at the time. This was the front page of a newspaper on the day after Queen Elizabeth II was crowned, in June 1953.

## What types of evidence can we use?

There are many kinds of evidence to help you find out about the changes in Britain since the Second World War:

- artefacts – things that people made at the time that are still here today, such as cars, toys, or furniture
- public written records – such as birth certificates, newspapers, and magazines
- personal written evidence – letters or diaries
- books – for example, stories that were written in the past or studies that people have done on a particular time
- maps
- films
- music
- plays
- photographs and paintings.

You can also ask people who were there at the time. They can tell you about their lives, and what it was like to live through those times.

Things like televisions and clothes can tell us a lot about how things have changed.

# What are the changes in work and home life since 1948? When did these changes happen?

## Changes in workers

After the war, many people thought that life would get back to normal, with men at work and women looking after the home. However, women had got used to having jobs, and many married women wanted to continue working if they chose. In 1951, only one in every five women worked. By 1995, one in two, or half, of women had some kind of paid job.

## Changes in jobs

The kinds of jobs people did also changed. During the 1950s and 1960s the number of jobs in areas such as coal mining, shipbuilding and fishing, fell. New industries grew, such as making cars and electrical items. From the 1970s, even more people were working in offices, and fewer in **factories**.

Computers also changed the way people work. Many jobs that used to be done by hand can now be done using computers. Computers also allow some people to work from home.

Our homes have changed a lot since 1948. This kitchen from the 1970s was very different from a typical 1950s kitchen, but it still looks old-fashioned today.

## Homes

In the 1950s and 1960s homes became a lot more comfortable, with central heating and items such as fridges and televisions. In the 1970s and 1980s people bought new inventions such as dishwashers and videos. More people also decided to buy their own home rather than to rent a house.

## Families

By the 1990s, more marriages ended in divorce. People often got married again, so more children had step-parents, but many had only one parent. Many women worked for longer, had babies when they were older, or had no babies at all.

## See for yourself

### Albert Docks, Liverpool

The Albert Docks in Liverpool were built in 1845, when Britain's sea trade was flourishing. The large warehouses stored goods that used the port. During the 20th century this sea trade declined, and the docks became deserted. Then, in the 1980s the Albert Docks were developed as a new tourist attraction. The warehouses are now shops, and cafés line the waterside. There is a museum about Liverpool's most famous musicians, The Beatles. This regeneration has created new kinds of jobs in the area, and brought a new prosperity.

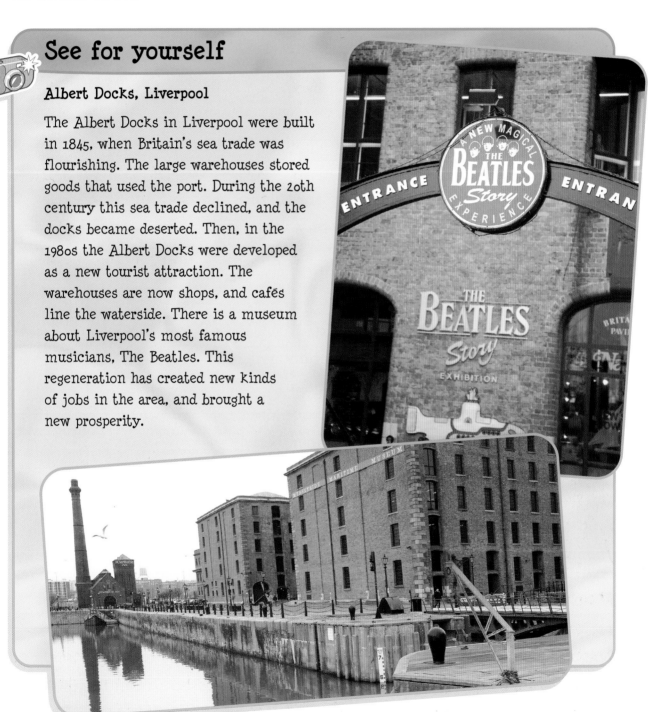

## What are the changes in technology and popular culture since 1948? When did these changes happen?

From 1948, **technology** changed the way people lived. The speed of this change increased from the 1980s. A popular culture also developed. This meant ideas, entertainments, and activities that everyone could enjoy.

### Computers

Computers changed the way people lived. **Microprocessors** were invented in 1971 to power computers. They were soon in all kinds of machines, from microwave ovens to fridges that can defrost themselves. Computers in **factories** replaced many jobs previously done by people, but they also created new jobs in offices.

### Communication

After the war, more people installed a telephone at home. The first mobile phone was made in 1979. Early mobiles were large and expensive, and only a few people had one until the 1990s. Today, many people use them. Now, the Internet means that anyone with a computer can keep in touch with others, learn, and even shop without leaving home. Many people also communicate by email on their computers.

By the late 1990s mobile phones, which use satellites to make their connections, meant that people could keep in touch with other people all over the world.

### Medicine and space

Technology also led to developments in medicine. Laser light beams made operations less complicated. New equipment allowed doctors to see inside our bodies, so they could **diagnose** and treat illnesses better. Technology also led to our exploration of space. The first person landed on the Moon in 1969.

## Home entertainment

Developments in technology have meant big changes in the way we entertain ourselves at home. Radio was the most important home entertainment until people began to buy televisions in the 1950s. At first people could only watch black and white programmes on TV, but by the 1970s colour was available. More channels to watch and the invention of the video and then the DVD, gave people much more choice over what they watched.

Fashions in music changed quickly. In the mid 1970s a new kind of music called **punk** was popular. Punk music attacked all kinds of authority, such as the government, school and parents. Punks wanted to shock people with the way they looked.

## Popular culture

The experience of living through the Second World War helped to break down barriers between people from different social classes. The radio also helped in this. All kinds of people found they could talk about the same things. During the 1950s and 1960s this popular culture grew. It was helped by new fashions and new machines that could bring television and music into everyone's homes.

## The Beatles

The Beatles (1960–1970) were the first British pop group to become a hit in the USA. The Beatles were John Lennon, Paul McCartney, George Harrison, and Ringo Starr. They had their first hit record with 'Love Me Do'. People loved it and Beatlemania hit Britain. After that The Beatles had many hits in Britain and the USA. From 1965 on, The Beatles found it harder to keep going. People wanted more hit songs but the band, especially John Lennon and Paul McCartney, began to like different types of music. The Beatles split up in 1970.

# What are the changes in Britain's population since 1948? When did these changes happen?

Since the 1930s, Britain's population has changed in size, **ethnic** mix, and age mix.

## Getting bigger

In 1931, the population of Britain was 46 million. In 1996, it was about 58 million. Today the growth of the population is slowing down. This is because fewer babies are being born. The population figures also take in the numbers of people **emigrating** from and **immigrating** to Britain.

## Getting more varied

In the 1930s, there were not many people living in Britain who were not white or who were not Christian. After the war, many immigrants came to Britain. By 1990, almost one in ten of the people living in Britain were non-white or of mixed race.

At first, most people did not mind immigrants moving to Britain. There were enough jobs for everyone. As time passed, more and more immigrants came from **Commonwealth** countries. Some white British people began to get upset. Sometimes immigrants were attacked. Laws were made to stop people attacking people of other ethnic backgrounds who lived in Britain.

Britain's society now includes people from many ethnic backgrounds. People from the same background sometimes gather in one part of a city. This is Brick Lane in London. Many Indians and Bangladeshis run restaurants and shops here.

## Getting older

In 1931, fewer children were being born and people were living longer. After the war, people began to have more children and there was a 'baby boom'. By the 1980s and 1990s, fewer children were being born again. Thanks to the National Health Service and new medicines, people were living even longer. Britain had more old people than young people. The drop in the number of younger people and rise of older people is still happening.

After people retire from work aged 65, they can expect to live for many more years. Some of them have time and money to spend. More older people now take holidays and buy new goods.

## Exploring further

Use the Heinemann Explore CD-ROM, or visit the website to find out more about:

- immigrants to Britain in the 1950s. Look in 'Exploring, Everyday Life, Moving in, moving out' and 'Pictures'.

- statistics about the different ethnic groups in Britain in 1990. Look in 'Written Sources'.

## Claudia Jones

Claudia Jones (1915–1964) was born in Trinidad but she moved to New York in the USA when she was eight years old. She became a journalist and worked hard to get black people treated more equally, especially black women. In the 1950s Claudia moved to Britain. In 1958, she set up the first big newspaper for West Indians and other black people living in Britain. It was called the *West Indian Gazette*. In 1959, she set up the first West Indian carnival in Notting Hill, in London. She ran the carnival until 1964. Claudia also set up a group to help people work together to stop anti-black feelings. This group was called the Coloured People's Progressive Association. In 1962, the **government** wanted to pass a law that would reduce the number of immigrants allowed into Britain. Claudia did not like this act. She worked so hard to stop it that she made herself ill. Claudia died in 1964, aged just 49. The Notting Hill Carnival is still held every year.

# What links and connections can we make between the changes in British life since 1948?

A good way to show how different changes link up is to make a wall chart that lists the questions you have asked and gives very short, simple answers. Then you can join the questions that have connections with different coloured marker-pen lines or with coloured string. For example, you may have asked the question, 'What changes in technology have there been?' The answer could be, 'Jet planes'. You may also have asked, 'How did everyday life change?' and answered with, 'People flew overseas for holidays'. This answer can be linked to 'Jet planes'.

## Many answers

When thinking about the most important changes and how they are linked, there is not one correct answer or set of answers. You are choosing what you think. As long as you have a good reason for your choice, your answer is right.

You will find many links because one change usually sets off other changes. For example, changes in work led to changes in families and in the population. Changes in technology led to changes in just about everything.

The changes in our lives since 1948 have given most people more free time, more money to spend and more choice. Today we often shop in large shopping centres like Birmingham's Bullring above, rather than in small local shops. Some things have remained popular from before 1930. Watching sport, especially football, is still a national pastime.

Ray Lomas, from Maidstone, in Kent, feels that holidays abroad have changed a lot since he was a boy.

*I remember when package holidays to Spain first came out. The family went on a package for two weeks. My dad said never again. They came back bright red and peeling, with upset tummies from the foreign food. I loved it, but my baby sister was too hot and it was hard to get food she or my parents would eat. Because then, abroad was different, really foreign and not many of the locals spoke English. We asked them to go with us to Torremolinos a few years ago. They were stunned by the difference. They loved it. It was Eastbourne (where they went every year after the package disaster), only sunny. The people spoke English. You could get fish and chips and Dad's favourite beer. They're going back next year. We aren't. We only went there that year because we knew they'd love it. We like to look for places that are still different from England – they're getting harder and harder to find.*

This was written by Michio Kaku in *Visions*, published in 1998.

*In many ways the impact of the Internet is like the invention of moveable type in the 1450s, which meant large numbers of books could be printed for the first time. Before this there were only about 30,000 books in all of Europe. Only a few people owned books or could read. Books were a luxury and a tool that were jealously guarded. The Internet takes another step towards spreading information widely and quickly.*

## Exploring further

Use the Heinemann Explore CD-ROM or website to find out more about:

- changes in the city of Canterbury since 1948, a good example of the changes in British cities. Look in 'Digging Deeper, Modern Britain'.

- two key figures of the late 20th century, Bill Gates and Richard Branson. Look in 'Digging Deeper'.

# Timeline

| | |
|---|---|
| 1936 | The BBC demonstrates television at the Radio Exhibition, London |
| 1937 | Frozen food such as peas and asparagus is on sale for the first time |
| 1938 | German forces take over Austria and the German-speaking parts of Czechoslovakia |
| 1939 | German forces take over the rest of Czechoslovakia. Britain promises to defend Poland if Germany attacks it |
| 1 Sep 1939 | German forces attack Poland. |
| 3 Sep 939 | Britain, France, New Zealand, and Australia declare war on Germany |
| 8 Jan 1940 | Food **rationing** begins |
| 7 Dec 1941 | Japan bombs US ships in Pearl Harbor |
| 8 May 1945 | VE Day: the end of the war in Europe |
| 14 Aug 1945 | Japan **surrenders**, after **atomic bombs** are dropped on Hiroshima and Nagasaki |
| 1948 | The National Health Service (NHS) is set up to give everyone access to free medical treatment |
| 1958 | The first stretch of motorway (8 miles of the M1) opens |
| 1962 | The Beatles have their first hit record with 'Love Me Do' |
| 1966 | Barclays Bank introduces the first ever **credit** card |
| 1968 | A new law makes it illegal to refuse someone a job because of their race or colour |
| 1972 | The world's first 'test tube baby' is born in England |
| 1973 | Britain joins the European Economic Community (EEC) |
| 1975 | A new laws says that boys and girls must receive the same education opportunities, and that all jobs must be open to both men and women |
| 1979 | Margaret Thatcher becomes the first woman Prime Minister |
| 1990 | Personal computers are now common in schools, offices, and homes |
| 1994 | The Channel Tunnel between Britain and France opens |
| 1998 | The people of Scotland and Wales vote in favour of having their own Parliaments to decide local affairs |

# See for yourself

### Albert Docks, Liverpool
An excellent example of how a site associated with old industry has been regenerated in modern times to bring new wealth and jobs. The docks have shops, museums, and cafés.

### Imperial War Museum, London
The museum has a wealth of exhibits on the Second World War, covering both the armed forces and the home front. A major new exhibition covers the 1940s house and all aspects of life in Britain through the war.

### Imperial War Museum, Duxford
This important aviation museum has one of the finest collections of tanks, military vehicles, and naval exhibits in the country. The site played a vital role in the Second World War, firstly as an RAF fighter station and later as an American fighter base.

### Imperial War Museum North, The Quays, Manchester
The museum has extensive displays exploring the home front in the north. Subjects covered include women's work in wartime.

### Bletchley Park, Milton Keynes
Bletchley Park was home to the famous codebreakers of the Second World War and the birthplace of modern computing and communications. You can see the famous Enigma Machine, the main coding device for the German armed forces which they believed to be unbreakable. Also see 'Colossus', the world's first ever semi-programmable computer.

### Dover Castle, Kent
Visit the network of underground tunnels beneath Dover Castle where, in May 1940, an operation was put into force to evacuate thousands of British and French soldiers trapped on the beaches of Dunkirk across the sea in northern France.

### Churchill Museum and Cabinet War Rooms, London
As bombs rained down on London in 1940, Winston Churchill and his War Cabinet met in these underground Cabinet War Rooms. Today visitors can see them just as them looked during the war years.

# Glossary

**air raid** attack by enemy aircraft, particularly bombing

**allies** people or countries working or fighting together.

**Allies** all the countries that fought against Germany in the Second World War

**Anderson shelter** shell made of a sheet of corrugated iron buried in a garden to use as an air raid shelter

**atomic bomb** very powerful kind of bomb, dropped on the Japanese cities of Hiroshima and Nagasaki in 1945

**Blitz** short for the German word 'blitzkrieg' meaning 'lightning war', used to describe the constant bombing raids on Britain by the German Luftwaffe from September 1940 to May 1941

**census** count of all the people in the country on a particular day

**Chancellor** in Germany, the equivalent of the Prime Minister

**Commonwealth** international association that is made up of Britain and countries that were previously part of the British Empire

**communications** facilities like roads, railways, and telephone lines

**credit** buying something, and not having to pay until later

**death camp** place where thousands of people are murdered

**decade** a period of ten years

**diagnose** to work out what is medically wrong with a person

**dictator** ruler with complete power, especially one who has taken control by force

**emigrate** to leave one country to live permanently in another

**ethnic** relating to a particular population or racial group

**evacuate** to move people out of a place that has become or may become dangerous

**evacuee** someone who is evacuated

**factory** place where people use machines to help them manufacture, or make, a product

**gas mask** mask worn over the face to protect against gas dropped by the enemy in war

**government** people who run a country

**immigrate** to come to live in one country from another country, usually the one you were born in

**Land Army** most people in the Land Army were women, who were trained and then moved around the country to work on farms that needed extra workers

**Luftwaffe** German air force

**mine** bomb hidden under the ground or at sea

**MP** Member of Parliament

**Nazi Party** the ruling political party in Germany just before and during the Second World War

**parliament** elected people who make the laws of a country

**punk** a 1970s fashion in music and lifestyle. It was loud and rude and about rebelling against authority.

**rationing** fixing the amount of food, petrol, or other goods that people can buy

**refugees** people who have fled a place because of religious or political persecution there

**surrender** to admit defeat

**technology** using science for practical purposes

**United Nations** international group representing nearly all of the world's countries

# Index